Stories of Jewish Symbols

STORIES

BLOCH PUBLISHING COMPANY,
NEW YORK

EST. 1854

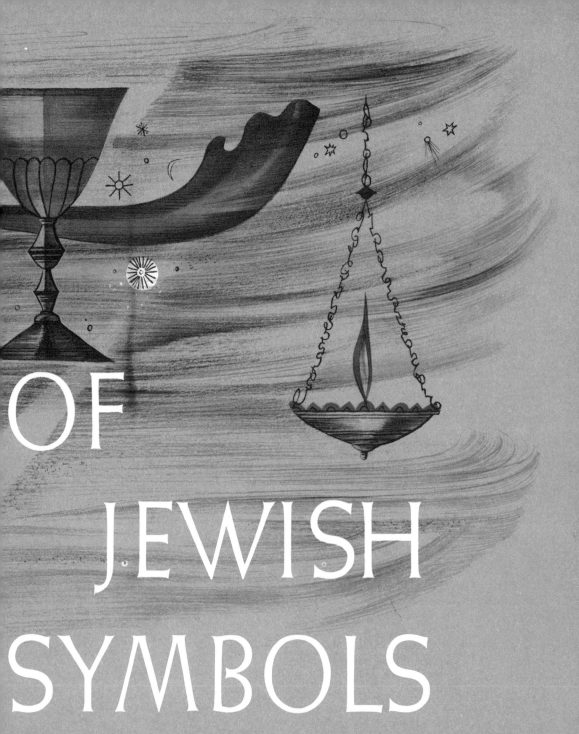

OF JEWISH SYMBOLS

by MOLLY CONE

Design and Illustration Siegmund Forst

Special thanks to
Jeanette Schrieber
for editorial and research assistance.

Contents

What is a Symbol ?

A symbol is something that stands for something else. You can usually see a symbol and sometimes even feel it. When you do, you are reminded of what it represents. A dove is a symbol. It stands for peace.

The American flag is a symbol. It stands for one nation, indivisible, with liberty and justice for all. Look at the red, white and blue flag and you see more than the stars and the stripes. You see that this country is your country.

The American flag is the oldest symbol our country has. Its meaning is strong and clear and sure.

It is the same with the symbols of our religion. Jewish symbols come from ancient times. "Ancient" means thousands of years ago. Judaism began with Abraham and Isaac and Jacob. It began with God's promise to Abraham to make his children into a great people. Every time a Jew looks at a symbol of his religion, he sees more than the object itself. He sees the ideas or things for which the symbol stands.

When the Shofar is blown at the High Holy Day services, the sound of the ram's horn takes us back to Bible times and Temple days. When we look upon the Tablets above the Ark in our synagogue, we can picture Moses carrying the Tablets of the Ten Commandments down a mountainside.

When we look at the Torah, it is not just an ancient scroll. We behold a parchment whose words have guided the lives of all our forefathers. The Eternal Light shining over the Ark, the Menorah nearby, are not just lights, but lights that speak to us soundlessly. They tell us that they lighted Jewish faces and Jewish hearts for thousands of years.

In the symbol designs on the Ark curtain, and the Torah mantle, and in the symbol patterns of stained glass windows, sculptures and carvings, we see more than beauty. For each symbol has a special meaning.

It is the same in our home. The Sabbath candles and the Friday night hallah, the matzah of Passover and the Hanukkah draydel—these are more than just candles, a loaf of bread, a dry cracker, and a toy that spins. Each object has a particular meaning.

This book is a guide to Jewish symbols and their meanings.

Every chapter will tell a story drawn from the treasury of Jewish tradition. After you have read the story, you will be introduced to a symbol and what it stands for.

By knowing more about our past and our present, you will become a better Jew and a better human being.

But first of all and most important, we hope you enjoy this book!

MEZUZAH

A Gift for a Gift

A king sent a gift to a man named Abba Arika.

It was a gift which would have overwhelmed most men. But not Abba Arika. He and the king had often talked together, and had become friends. They had even exchanged jokes.

The gift from the king which Abba Arika unwrapped before the startled gaze of his neighbors was a pearl.

"It is priceless!" whispered a merchant friend who turned it this way and that. "It is perfect," he added. "But what will you give in return?"

Abba Arika looked about his house. It was plain to see that nothing in his house was equal to the gift of the king.

"Naturally," pointed out the merchant, "the king will expect you to give him a gift of equal value."

Thoughtfully, Abba Arika's glance rested on his doorway. "I will send him a gift even more valuable," he said.

Shortly after, Abba Arika carried his gift to the king. It lay in his hand. It was a tiny wooden case, no bigger than the king's thumb.

The king looked at the small case in amazement. "I sent you a priceless gift," he said, "and you give me something worth almost nothing!"

"One is more valuable than the other," Abba Arika agreed. "But it is not the one you think. You sent me something which I must guard, but I give you something which will guard you—even when you sleep."

With a puzzled expression the king turned the small object over in his hand. Then he threw back his head and laughed loudly. "It is a joke!" he said.

Abba Arika shook his head. "It is not a joke; it is a Mezuzah."

מזוזה

9

. . . AND THE SYMBOL

Mezuzah is the Hebrew word for "doorpost." A Mezuzah is a small case of wood or metal containing a roll of parchment. Upon the tiny scroll we find two passages from *Deuteronomy* 6:5-9 and 11:13-21. They are in Hebrew, written in the manner of Torah script. The first is the famous passage which begins: HEAR, O ISRAEL, THE LORD OUR GOD, THE LORD IS ONE. The little scroll is rolled up so that the first word of the prayer, *Shema,* is at the top. Then it is fitted into the Mezuzah case.

Through a little opening in the case, the Hebrew word *Shaddai,* written on the back side of the parchment, may be seen. Shaddai means Almighty, and is another name for God.

The case is fastened to the right doorpost as directed in the Bible commandment—"You shall write them upon the doorposts of your house."

When we move into a new home, the first thing we do is fasten a Mezuzah to the upper part of the right doorpost of each room.

Every time we walk into our house or leave it, the Mezuzah fastened there at the doorway reminds us there is One God. It reminds us that each member of our family must be taught to honor the things our faith stands for: honesty and justice, mercy and kindness, generosity, and love, and peace.

What Abba Arika told the king was perfectly true. The wisdom found in the Mezuzah is more valuable even than pearls.

The Mezuzah at the doorpost of a house is a sign of God's presence. It announces that those who dwell within are proud members of the Jewish people and aware of our long and honorable heritage.

The Mezuzah says: "This is a Jewish home."

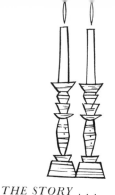

SABBATH CANDLES

The Secret Ingredient

A king who passed a poor Jewish home every night noted a strange thing. Every Friday night, a delicious smell came from the doorway of the little house.

One Friday night he had his servant knock at the door and demand a tax in the form of whatever was on the stove.

When the king reached his palace, he sat down at his table and dipped his spoon into the pot of soup that had been given to his servant. He put the spoon to his mouth and tasted. The soup was very good soup, to be sure, but it was not much different from the soup his own cook made.

"Bah!" he shouted. "This is not it at all!"

So the next Friday afternoon, when he again passed the house of the poor Jew, he stopped and knocked.

As soon as the door was opened, the delicious smell tickled his nose. "Mmmmm," he said. "What is that you are cooking?"

"It is a bit of meat for our Sabbath dinner," said the Jew.

Whereupon the king demanded it as a tax, and took it away with him. But when he got home, the meat tasted no different than the meat from his own kitchen.

Puzzled, the king decided that the next week when he would be passing the house of the Jew, he would demand that whatever it was that smelled so good be handed over at once.

The next week, after sundown, he knocked loudly at the door of the Jew.

"Tell me, what is it that smells so good in this house every Friday night?" he demanded.

The Jew looked about his small home. The Sabbath candles spread light over the dinner table. The freshly baked Hallahs lay ready under their napkin cover. The cup of wine stood nearby. As it was every Sabbath at this time, all work had been put away. Food for the next day had been prepared. The windows sparkled; the floor was swept clean. And his wife and children sat at the table with the glow of the Sabbath on their faces. It was true— a delicious aroma seemed to fill the house.

"It is the Sabbath spice," he said softly.

"Sabbath spice!" said the king. "Where does it grow?"

"It does not grow," said the Jew. "It is the Day of Rest, which we call the Sabbath. It begins when the Sabbath candles are lit."

**SABBATH
CANDLES**

14

When the candles are lit in a Jewish home on Friday evening, the light has a special meaning. It shines for the Sabbath. The lighting of the Sabbath candles is one of the oldest symbols of the Jewish faith.

This symbol reminds every Jew of the promise made to God at the foot of Mount Sinai. This promise was a covenant, an agreement between the Lord and the Jewish people—

"The children of Israel shall keep the Sabbath, to observe the Sabbath throughout their generations as a perpetual covenant. It is a sign between Me and the children of Israel forever . . . that you shall remember My commandments" (*Exodus* 20:8-11).

The Sabbath is God's gift to the Jewish people. God created the world in six days and on the seventh He rested. On this day we do as God did; we rest. Weekday worries, as well as work, are put away and forgotten on the Sabbath.

Rest on the Sabbath means doing something different from that which is done every day.

The Talmud notes the thoughts on Sabbath rest of three wise rabbis. One said the Sabbath day should be a day of pleasure. Another declared that the Sabbath day was meant for study. A third rabbi agreed with both of them. Those who study during the week shall rest and enjoy the Sabbath, he said. And those who do not study and learn during the week, will find their pleasure and rest in doing so on the Sabbath.

This day of rest begins at sundown every Friday, and ends when the stars come out on Saturday.

The lighting of the candles before sundown reminds everyone that the Sabbath is about to begin. It is the mother of the family who lights the candles and recites the prayer before the Sabbath begins. Shielding her eyes with her hands in order not to see the light until the prayer is said, she recites:

> Blessed art Thou, O Lord our God, King of the universe,
> Who hast made us holy by Thy laws and commanded us to kindle the Sabbath lights.

The light of the candles reminds the Jewish people to put away their daily work for one day, to think of God, to rest.

What the king in the old Sabbath tale could not take home with him was the peace of the Sabbath day. It had a fragrance all its own.

The light of the Sabbath candles is a symbol of the Jewish way of life.

The World and the Vineyard

THE STORY . . .

An old tale says that over every vineyard are the shadows of four animals—a lamb, a lion, a pig, and a monkey.

Before a man drinks wine, he is like the lamb, young and gentle.

When a man drinks a little wine, he is like the lion, strong and graceful.

When a man drinks much more than a little, he is like the pig, unpleasant to all.

And when he drinks far too much, he is like the monkey, who dances and chatters foolishly.

The Talmud says that the whole world is like a vineyard, for it offers both good and evil. The choice is up to man himself.

The wise men of the Talmud listed three things which help a man enjoy a good life. The first is the study of Torah. The second is being humble. And the third is a blessing over a cup of wine.

Wine grapes grew abundantly in ancient Israel. Even the poorest farmers were able to drink wine with their holiday meals. Since the Sabbath was the holiest as well as the happiest time of the week to our ancestors, the Sabbath dinner began with wine. In later times the Kiddush, or blessing over wine, began to be said at the synagogue because wayfarers were lodged in the house of prayer. Thus they were able to hear the blessing over wine.

. . . AND THE SYMBOL

In Jewish homes there is a special cup for the Sabbath or holiday wine. It is called the Kiddush cup.

The wine cup is filled by the head of the household at the Sabbath table. He chants the Kiddush.

Every man, no matter how poor he is during the week, is king in his home on the Sabbath. He is like a lion who knows his strength. At the Sabbath table, he looks around at his family with pride, and to their future with new hope. The cup of wine with which he says a blessing for the Sabbath becomes a cup of joy. It reminds him that as long as men are free to choose good over evil, they are masters of their lives. As he drinks from the cup of joy, he thinks of all this, and in doing so, he makes holy the Sabbath.

The Kiddush cup is a symbol of holiness and joy.

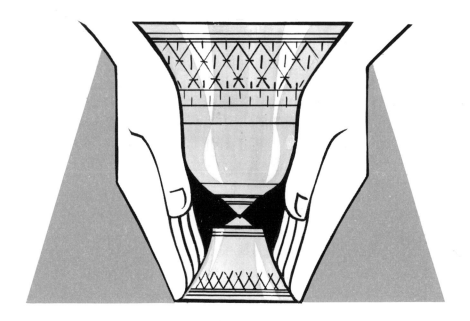

SABBATH HALLAH

The Riddle

THE STORY . . .

"Would you like to hear a riddle?" asked one traveler of another as they passed through a small village.

"In the middle of last week, I stopped here at dinner time, at the house of a poor man. On his table was a poor man's dinner—dark bread and potatoes.

"At the end of the week, I stopped again, and again I sat down to dinner in the same house. But this time it was the table of a king—for upon it was white bread, and fish, and vegetables, and meat. Now, can you explain that?"

The man sitting next to him shook his head in wonder.

A third traveler in the carriage leaned forward and tapped the speaker on the knee. "May I ask, was there on the table a twisted, white breadloaf?"

The first speaker nodded.

"Then I can explain it," said the man. "For it was a Jewish house!"

. . . AND THE SYMBOL

No other meal of the week in a Jewish house is like the Sabbath meal. This has been true for as long as Jews have kept the Sabbath. No matter how poor the Jew, the Friday night and Sabbath day meals are special meals. And one difference that is readily marked is the presence of special loaves of twisted white bread.

In ancient times, on weekdays, only one cooked dish made up each meal. For the Sabbath, two or more dishes were prepared. On weekdays ordinary, roughly-milled bread was good enough. But on the Sabbath, only white bread was served.

The Sabbath loaf is called Hallah. Two loaves are part of the ceremony of the Sabbath meals. The two Hallot are known as *lehem mishneh* (double bread). They remind

us that the Israelites, while in the wilderness on their way
to the Promised Land, gathered on Friday a double portion of *manna* to last them for two days, because on the
Sabbath they were not permitted to gather *manna*, the
food that descended to them from the skies.

The coverlet on the Hallot recalls the dew which
covered the *manna* every morning.

The Hallah served on the Sabbath is a symbol. It is a
reminder of the difference between meals served during
the workaday week and those served on the Day of Rest.

HAVDALAH

The Ending of the Song

Wise King Solomon looked upon the two angry men before him.

"I have written a beautiful song," said one, "and now this man says it is he who wrote it."

"But I did write it!" said the second man. "I finished my song and, when my back was turned, this man stole it from me. He is telling everyone it is his!"

King Solomon gave the problem some thought. "Each of you go home and write an ending verse to the song," he said. "Then bring what you have written to me."

The two men did so. And the king looked upon the verses and compared first one, and then the other, with the song. Then he set the verses down and smiled.

"You are the true composer of the hymn," he said to the second man. "For the ending of your song harmonizes with the beginning."

. . . AND THE SYMBOL

In just this way does the ending of the Sabbath day echo its beginning. Its special feeling lasts until three stars are seen in the evening sky.

The end of the Sabbath (and of other festivals) is celebrated with a Havdalah ceremony. Havdalah is the Hebrew word for separation. The Havdalah blessing separates the holy day from the weekday.

A wine cup, a candle, and a spice box are the special religious objects used for the Havdalah.

The wine cup is filled to the brim. The cup of wine is a symbol of a week to come, brimful of blessings.

The candle, twisted of several strands, is lit. The Havdalah candle is made up of many strands to symbolize many kinds of God's light. It is a symbol of all light which God created—the light of His laws, as well as the light of the sun and the moon.

The spice box may be filled with a mixture of cloves, nutmeg and bay leaves. Often the box is made to look like a tower, a *migdal,* and is sometimes called that.

The head of the family says a blessing over wine, spices, and light. The blessing over light reminds us that light was the first thing God created. The spices have replaced the incense-burning which took place at festive events in olden times. The family breathes the aroma of the spices and hopes for a week that will be just as fragrant.

The ceremony is over. The Sabbath is over. The symbols of Havdalah—the candle, the wine, the spice box—have helped us to see and feel the wonders of our Almighty, Who made a difference between light and dark, holy and ordinary, Sabbath and weekday.

TORAH

The Fish Who Were Afraid

THE STORY ...

TORAH

22

Rabbi Akiba sat on a river bank teaching the Torah to his students. At that time the Roman rulers did not permit Jews to study the Torah. But Rabbi Akiba paid no attention to this law.

"Beware!" said a passerby. "If you go on with the study of the Torah, they will make you suffer for it!"

Rabbi Akiba looked up from the book. "Have you given up the study of the Torah?" he asked in wonder.

"Of course!" said the Jew. "I'm no fool!"

Rabbi Akiba turned his head and thoughtfully studied the fish swimming in the river.

"Let me tell you a story," he said, "and let these students decide who is right, you or I."

The stranger darted a glance over his shoulder to make sure that no one was spying, and then sat down. The students listened.

Rabbi Akiba began. "Once, while walking beside the river, a fox saw some fish darting wildly about in the stream.

" 'What are you so afraid of?' called the fox.

" 'We are afraid of the fishermen's nets,' said the fish. 'The river is full of them.'

"The fox licked his lips greedily. The fish were sleek and fat. He was sorry that he himself did not have a net. He suggested, 'Why don't you jump out on dry land and live as I do?' His eyes gleamed. 'No nets to fear,' he added.

"The young fish began to move closer to the bank. It was true. As far as they could see, there were no nets on the green bank. No nets at all.

" 'Wait!' gulped one of the fish to the others. 'If there are things to be afraid of where it is natural for us to live, isn't there much more to be afraid of on dry land where we cannot even breathe?' "

"Ah-h-h," said Rabbi Akiba's students with quick smiles.

"Eh-h-h?" said the man. He scowled. He wasn't sure he saw the point.

Rabbi Akiba said, "Just so it is with us who study the Torah. Without the Torah we would be like fish on dry land. We could not breathe. We could not live! If we suffer while studying Torah, how much more would we suffer if we did not study!"

TORAH

24

Torah is the Hebrew word for "teaching" or "law." The Torah is the law we live by. It is the law we received through Moses on Mount Sinai.

When our ancestors first began to write down the Torah, they wrote it on parchment made of the hide of certain animals. The Torah is still written that way today. It must be written by hand and attached to two wooden rollers, called "Trees of Life."

The Scroll of the Torah contains the Five Books of Moses. These books are named *Genesis, Exodus, Leviticus, Numbers,* and *Deuteronomy.* In Hebrew these books are called: *B'ray-shis, Shemot, Vayikra, Bemidbar* and *Devarim.*

Genesis tells of the creation of the world. Its chief purpose is to tell us how God wants us to live in His world. *Exodus* is the story of the Hebrews in Egypt, and their forty years of wandering in the wilderness. It sings the praises of freedom from slavery and reminds us that God wants all men to enjoy freedom. *Leviticus* takes up the problems of Jewish nationhood. *Numbers* tells how the children of Israel lived from the time they left Mount Sinai until they reached the borders of Canaan. *Deuteronomy* follows the Israelites until the death of Moses, and reviews the Laws of the Torah.

Many people today say "Torah" when they mean all of Jewish holy learning. They mean not only the Five Books of Moses, but the writings of the prophets, the sages, rabbis, scholars and teachers—over hundreds of years, all put together and all found in many books.

A different section of the Torah is read on every Sabbath and on holidays. And when the end is reached, the
Torah is rolled back and started over again. The end and
beinning take place on the holiday called Simhat Torah.

When the Torah is not being read, a mantle protects
it. The mantle or cover has two openings for the rollers
or handles of the Torah Scroll to go through.

Mantle covers are usually of royal purple or rich red
or deep blue, but on the High Holy Days, the most solemn
time of the year, the Torah wears a white mantle to symbolize purity.

Over the Torah mantle hangs a shield or "Hoshen," much like the breastplates worn by the priests in the ancient Temple of Jerusalem. A pointer, too, hangs from a chain over the Torah mantle. It is called "Yad" and is a silver hand with a pointing finger. The "Yad" is used to mark the place in the Scroll for the reader.

A favorite Torah ornament is a crown. Sometimes the "Keter Torah," or Torah crown, fits over both handles; sometimes, there is a smaller crown, one for each handle. The smaller crowns are called "Rimmonim." The Keter Torah reminds the Jewish people of the holiness of the Laws in the Torah.

The Torah is always treated with deep respect. Before and after the Sabbath portion is read, blessings are recited.

Rabbi Akiba was right when he persisted in studying the Torah even though he might suffer for doing so. For he was wise enough to know that a Jew who does not live by God's law is like a fish that tries to live out of water.

He knew that the Torah is the most precious possession of the Jewish people.

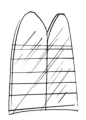

LUHOTH

(Tablets of the Ten Commandments)

The Promise

THE STORY . . .

Four young men, out to seek their fortunes, came to a field. The sun beat down, and the field lay waiting to be planted.

The young men saw that the field was divided into ten sections. And the earth in each was rich and black.

The king who owned the field rode by. When he saw them admiring the earth, he stopped.

"I will give this land to the one who promises to take care of it," he said. "Will you till it?" he asked one of the four men.

This young man was tall and strong but he had no appetite for hard work. "Not me!" he said quickly. "There are easier ways to win one's fortune."

"Not me!" said the second young man. "I left home because I didn't want to be a farmer."

"Don't look at me!" said the third young man. "I'm on my way!" And he started off down the road.

The king turned to the fourth. "And you?" he asked. "Will you take this field ,and till it?"

Now this one was the smallest of the four and the poorest. He had no home to return to, and no friend to welcome him. He looked with longing at the big field. He thought of the barley he could raise, and the fruits and the vegetables. If only he could till it well, it would take care of him all the rest of his life.

"I will do it!" he said.

The king looked closely at him. "If you take it you must give me your promise to use all of its ten sections!"

The young man looked again. It was a very large field, and though some sections were level and promised easy tilling, some were very steep and rocky. He took a long, deep breath. "I will till it all," he said. "I give you my promise."

In just this way did the Israelites accept the Ten Commandments from the Lord.

After following Moses out of Egypt and wandering in the wilderness they came to Mount Sinai where the Lord offered them the Ten Commandments. The wanderers took them and promised to keep them. They accepted God's Laws for themselves and their families, their children and their children's children forever after. For the Israelites knew that the Commandments would be the source of their strength all their days.

The Ten Commandments, in Hebrew *Aseret Hadibrot,* became our law.

When Moses carried the Tablets down the mountainside, it is said that the words blazed like fire. When Moses read them out to the people, the Commandments burned into their hearts and their minds.

You can find the Ten Commandents in the Bible (*Exodus* 20):

I am the Lord your God who brought you out of the land of Egypt . . .

You shall have no other gods before me.

You shall not take the name of the Lord your God in vain.

Remember the Sabbath day and keep it holy . . .

Honor your father and your mother.

You shall not murder.

You shall not commit adultery.

You shall not steal.

You shall not bear false witness against your neighbor.

You shall not covet your neighbor's house . . . or anything that is your neighbor's.

These Ten Commandments became the foundation not only of our religion but of the moral law of all civilized nations. If all the people on the earth were to live by them, the world would be empty of evil and full of goodness.

Today the Tablets of the Law are placed above the Ark in our synagogue. Only the first two words of each of the Commandments are usually shown on the Tablets. Sometimes, instead of the words, the first ten letters of the Hebrew alphabet appear. These stand for the Hebrew numbers one to ten.

The Tablets of the Law are a symbol. They remind all who look upon them that the Jewish way of life began with the Ten Commandments and a promise made between God and man.

TALLIT

The Prayer Shawl

THE STORY ...

A boy, studying for his Bar Mitzvah asked, "Rabbi, what do you do before you pray?"

The rabbi answered, "I pray that when I pray it may be with all my heart."

...AND THE SYMBOL

It is to help him pray with all his heart that a Jew wraps himself in a prayer shawl.

The prayer shawl a Jew puts about his shoulders when he prays is called a "Tallit." It recalls the style of the upper garment worn in ancient Palestine. In those days the rabbis wore special robes as a sign of distinction. When Jews spread to other lands, the Tallit came to be used for religious services.

The Tallit had a special meaning. The Torah told the children of Israel to "make a fringe upon the corners of your garments, so that you may look upon it and remember all the commandments of the Lord." This is found in the *Book of Numbers*, 15:38-39.

So the ancient Jew wore a large shawl with fringes. The fringes were knotted at the four corners, and in the fringes was a thread of special blue. The blue was made from a secret formula by the people of Acre in Palestine.

But the secret of this blue dye was lost when Jerusalem was destroyed by the Romans. Today, fringes of the Tallit are white.

The fringes are called "Tzitzit" in Hebrew, and are made of threads of the same material as the Tallit. A Tallit has blue or black stripes.

When we were driven out of our land 2,000 years ago we went to many different places to live. Each country had its own style of clothing. The Jews began to dress like the neighbors and wore the Tallit only for prayer.

When the Tallit was no longer worn for every day, a smaller garment with fringes was worn instead, under the clothes. It was known as "Tallit Katan," a small Tallit, or "Arba Kanfot."

Without a country of their own, the Jews looked upon the wearing of the Tallit as a symbol of the time when they had their own country. When Israel became again a Jewish State in 1948, the blue and white colors of the Tallit were chosen for the striped flag of the State of Israel.

The Tallit is worn in the synagogue during morning services, and also at Sabbath and festival services. Usually a Bar Mitzvah boy wears a Tallit in the synagogue. But some men do not wear the prayer shawl until after marriage.

The Tallit helps the worshiper feel ready for praying. To those who wear it, it is a symbol of respect for prayer. The fringes are a reminder of all God's commandments.

TEFILLIN

How to Remember

THE STORY . . .

A rabbi asked one of his students to tell him how many commandments there were in the whole Torah.

The boy frowned. "I forget," he mumbled.

The rabbi said, "Then tell me the answer to another question. How many ears do you have?"

Surprised, the boy answered, "Two, of course."

"And how do you remember you have two ears?" asked the rabbi.

The boy grinned. "Because my ears are part of me," he said.

The rabbi smiled. "Well, what you must do now is study the commandments until they are part of you."

. . . AND THE SYMBOL

Great care has always been taken by our people to remember the commandments and to make them part of us. One of the ways which helped us remember came directly from the Bible.

To remember all God's commandments, the Torah tells us (in *Deuteronomy, 6:8*) to "bind them as a sign on your hand and let them serve as a symbol on your forehead."

From the word *T'filah*, or "prayer," comes *Tefillin*, or "phylacteries." Each of the two Tefillin is a little square box of parchment with a long strap attached. One box, called the "Shel Rosh," is worn above the forehead. The other, the "Shel Yad," is worn on the upper left arm. The box worn on the forehead lies close to the mind; the box tied to the arm points to the heart.

The head-piece has the letter *Shin*   stamped on it. The strap of the head-piece is tied in back into a knot shaped like a *Daled*   The knot of the arm-piece forms the letter *Yud*   The three Hebrew letters spell *Shaddai,* or "Almighty."

When a Jewish boy reaches the age of thirteen, he is expected to put on Tefillin during morning weekday prayers. (Reform Jews do not observe this law.)

The Tefillin are a symbol of the closeness of the Jewish people with the Creator.

TWELVE TRIBES

Twelve Brothers

THE STORY . . .

Once there was a man named Jacob. He had twelve sons. He loved them all, but he could see that they were not equal in their ways.

Benjamin was the gentlest, and Judah the strongest. Reuben was weak, and both Simeon and Levi were stubborn. Zebulun was sturdy as a ship, and Issachar hardworking. Dan was crafty, and Gad more a follower than a leader. Asher was slow and Naphtali swift, and Joseph was wise.

Before Jacob died, he called his sons together, and he talked to them and blessed them. With his dimming eyes he looked far into the future and he said he saw each of them as heads of the twelve tribes of Israel. What he dreamed for them is told in the *Book of Genesis* 49:1-27— and it came true many years later.

For after they came out of the land of Egypt, the Israelites were divided by Moses into Twelve Tribes. Each tribe took its name from one of the sons of Jacob. The Tribe of Levi was not counted as one of the twelve, for Moses selected it to be the one responsible for the Tabernacle. The Tribe of Joseph was divided between his two sons, Ephraim and Manasseh.

. . . AND THE SYMBOL

Today each of the Twelve Tribes is remembered by a symbol. Here are the names of the Tribes and their symbols:

Reuben	Mandrake plant
Simeon	City-gate of Shechem
Judah	Lion
Dan	Serpent
Naphtali	Doe

Gad	Camp tents
Asher	Olive tree
Issachar	Sun and stars
Zebulun	Ship
Manassah	Unicorn
Ephraim	Fish
Benjamin	Wolf

Sometimes, Manassah and Ephraim are not shown in seals of the Twelve Tribes. Instead we have Levi (symbol: breastplate of the High Priest) and Joseph (symbol: sheaf of grain).

In olden days each Tribe used its emblem as identification. The emblems are seen often today in synagogue architecture.

The symbols of the Twelve Tribes remind us of our ancient and colorful beginnings as a nation.

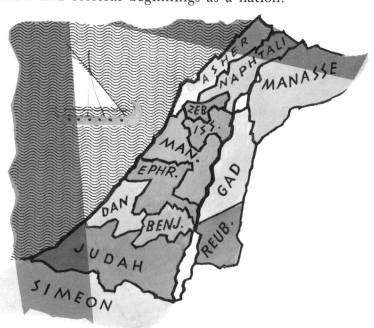

ARON HA-KODESH

(Holy Ark)

The Old Man and the Fig Tree

THE STORY . . .

A king passed a very old man planting a fig tree.

"Old man!" called the king. "Why do you work so hard to plant a tree that will not bear fruit for many years? Do you expect to live long enough to eat the figs from this tree?" And the king smiled at his own joke.

The old man looked down at his old legs which had carried him about for almost a hundred years, and then he looked at the roots of the young tree. The figs from this tree would be truly fine ones, he thought.

He smiled. "Perhaps I won't eat the figs, but my grandchildren will," he said. "Didn't my forefathers plant trees for me? Shouldn't I do the same for my children's children?" And he went back to his work without another word.

. . . AND THE SYMBOL

Like the old man who planted a tree to bear fruit for his children, the Israelites built an Ark to carry God's words to the coming generations.

They made the Ark of acacia wood, and built it so that it would be easy to carry on two poles. And because it would bear a precious burden, they lined it with gold, and made it beautiful. When they had finished, at each end of the Ark was a cherub—the figure of a childlike angel—for what was within the Ark was to be guarded for all children to come.

Into this Ark the Israelites placed the stone tablets of the Ten Commandments. They called this box with its holy treasure, the "Aron Ha-Kodesh," the Holy Ark.

The Ark went with them all the forty years they wandered in the wilderness. And when they reached the

Promised Land, and built the First Temple to God, the Ark was set in the holiest of holy places. Of all the sacred objects in the Temple, the Holy Ark was the most important.

It has always been so.

In every synagogue today, the holiest part is the Ark. For this is where the Torah, God's law, is kept.

In this country, the Aron Ha-Kodesh is usually built into the synagogue wall facing east. East is the direction of Jerusalem and Jerusalem is where the Ancient First and Second Temples were built.

All Jews face Jerusalem when they pray. No matter where they are, they are praying together. They are saying the prayers of their faith which began with the laws of God.

The curtain over the opening of the Holy Ark is called a "Parokhet." Often silver or gold threads spell out on it these words in Hebrew—"I have always set the Lord before me."

Many Holy Arks today have doors instead of curtains. Often the curtains or doors are decorated in symbol designs of the Tablets of the Law, the Lions of Judah, the Crown of the Law, the Star of David or another.

The Ark is like the tree which the old man planted for his grandchildren to enjoy. For the Ark holds the fruits of wisdom for every new generation.

The Holy Ark is a symbol. It reminds every Jew that he is part of a people whose law began with an ancient Ark and Two Tablets of stone.

NER TAMID

(Eternal Light)

The Rabbi and the Robber

THE STORY . . .

There was once an innkeeper who always awakened his guests before daylight and sent them on their way. But he would carefully give them the wrong directions, and send them over a lonely road where a band of robbers waited. The loot was later divided between the robbers and the innkeeper.

A rabbi happened to stop at the inn. And the innkeeper, with an eye on the rabbi's good coat and his well-fed donkey, shook him awake before daylight.

"But the sun has not risen!" said the rabbi.

The innkeeper smiled craftily. "You will be well on your way before the heat of the day. Come, I will show you the best way to go."

"I cannot go before *ki-tov* comes," said the rabbi, closing his eyes.

The innkeeper shook him again. "You did not tell me you were waiting for someone. When will he come?"

"Soon," said the rabbi, his eyes closed.

Several times the innkeeper went out to see whether anyone named Kitov had arrived. But no one at all was in sight.

When daylight came, the rabbi got up, smiled at the innkeeper, and climbed on his donkey.

"But I thought you were waiting for this person called "Kitov," said the innkeeper, disappointed that daylight had interfered with his plans to rob the man.

"But ki-tov is here," said the rabbi.

The innkeeper looked around the empty courtyard in surprise.

"It is written that God called the light of day, 'ki-tov,'"
said the rabbi. "I travel with God, and wait for the light
of day, ki-tov, for it is good." And with a wave of his
hand, the rabbi went safely on his way.

. *AND THE SYMBOL*

At the very beginning, the Torah says, God said: 'Let
there be light.' And there was light." The light became
the day.

In the Torah, God called the light "good," ki-tov,
and ever since that time, light has been the best of all
things to men. People speak of the *light* of knowledge
when they talk of education. They speak of the *light* of
truth when they choose right over wrong. They speak
of the *light* of hope, for hope is always for good to come.

The Commandment is a lamp and the Law is a light,
a Proverb says. The Torah which the Jewish people received from God has always been the guiding light of their
lives.

From the time of the First Temple in Jerusalem, every
Jewish house of worship has had a Ner Tamid. *Ner* is
Hebrew for light, and *Tamid* means forever. Ner Tamid
means the ever-burning light. That is why it is called the
Eternal Light.

The Eternal Light has a special place in the temple or
synagogue. It hangs over the Holy Ark which holds the
Torah.

In the First Temple, a lamp containing pure olive oil
burned continually before the Ark. Today when a new
synagogue is dedicated, the most important ceremonies
are the placing of the Torah Scrolls in the Ark and the
lighting of the Ner Tamid.

Light to the Jewish people has always been a symbol of the goodness of life. But the Eternal Light hanging over the Ark has a special meaning. It says to the Jewish people that the Law of the Torah is a light and that it is good. The Jewish people believe that where there is light there is God. The Eternal Light is the symbol of the presence of God among us, of happiness, of the light that the synagogue gives.

MENORAH

Moonbeams in a Barrel

THE STORY . . .

The little town of Helm was inhabited by people who thought they were very, very wise.

One bright moonlit night, they gathered together to try to catch moonbeams in a barrel. They placed the barrel in the middle of the town square and when the full moon poured its rays into the barrel, they quickly covered it up, and tied down the cover, and went home to bed.

The next moonless dark night they gathered about the barrel and took off its cover. Much to their surprise, there was nothing in it at all!

How these people of Helm tried to capture light was certainly foolish, but that they wanted light was not foolish at all.

From the very beginning of time, people have tried to keep the light with them. Light was part of the creation of the world. Light made people feel closer to God.

. . . AND THE SYMBOL

In the time of Moses, the Israelites carried with them in their wanderings not only the Holy Ark with the Tablets of the Law, but a "Menorah."

Menorah is the Hebrew word for lamp. The Menorah was a lamp which gave our people light in their tabernacle as they prayed. It had seven branches. On each branch was a little cup which held oil. When the oil burned, the Menorah gave light. This first Menorah is described exactly in the *Book of Exodus,* 37:17.

Today a Menorah in our synagogue holds candles or is lit by electricity.

Some people believed that the seven branches of the Menorah stood for the seven days of the week. Seven was a sacred number in olden times.

In the First Temple built by King Solomon, it is said that there were ten Menorahs. In the Second Temple built hundreds of years later, history tells of one Menorah. It was of solid gold.

It was this Menorah which was carried off when the Temple was destroyed almost two thousand years ago. The Roman general Titus took it as a symbol of victory. It was carried to Rome on the shoulders of the captive Jews.

Today a reminder of that solid gold Menorah being carried to Rome may be seen in the city of Rome, Italy. The scene is cut into the stone of an old arch, called the Arch of Titus.

It is this Menorah, at one time a symbol of defeat, which the State of Israel took to be its symbol of victory. The Menorah pictured on the Arch of Titus in Rome became the official symbol of Israel when the Jewish State was established in 1948. Two thousand years had passed before that defeat was turned into glowing victory!

Today the Menorah appears on the seal of the State of Israel. The light of the Menorah is a symbol of the hope of the future of Israel.

But the Menorah is also a symbol to all Jews everywhere. This ancient lamp is found in synagogues throughout the world.

The light of the seven branches of the Menorah is a reminder that the Jewish faith has lived for thousands of years. The Menorah is accepted everywhere as the symbol of Judaism.

MAGEN DAVID

(Shield of David)

The Question

THE STORY . . .

Once someone asked, "Why do they call noodles, noodles?"

The answer came quickly. "They are long like noodles, aren't they? They are soft like noodles, aren't they? And they taste like noodles, don't they? So why shouldn't they be called noodles?"

This same kind of answer can be given to the question, "Why is a six-pointed star called a Jewish Star?"

No one really knows the answer. The six-pointed star can be traced back thousands of years.

At one time it was a sign of magic. In the chemistry of hundreds of years ago, this triangle   was the sign for fire, and this triangle   the sign for water. The star   was made by putting together the two symbols. It was a very ancient symbol known to the Egyptians, Hindus, Chinese, and Peruvians.

But why the six-pointed star became a favorite symbol of the Jews and a sign of Judaism, is a question not easily answered.

It is told that David's soldiers wore the star on their shields. That is when it became known as the Star of David, or "Magen David." Magen David is the Hebrew for shield of David, meaning emblem, or coat of arms.

Not very many years ago, the German Nazi tyrant, Adolph Hitler, tried to make the Jewish star a badge of shame. In his slaughter of the Jews of Europe, he ordered all Jews to wear a yellow Star of David. Hitler was defeated and the Star of David remained a badge of honor.

Today the Magen David, bounded by two blue stripes on a white background, waves on the flag of the State of Israel. The Star of David is seen on synagogues, and on objects inside the synagogue. It is seen on seals of Jewish organizations and institutions, and is a Zionist emblem. Wherever it appears, it is recognized as a proud symbol of an eternal people.

מגן דוד
47

LIONS OF JUDAH

The Fourth Son

THE STORY . . .

Judah was the fourth son of Jacob. Though Jacob loved all his twelve sons, he was filled with special admiration for Judah. For not only was Judah good, but he also had strength. He was strong as a lion's cub, his father liked to say.

Jacob predicted the future of his sons with care, saying to each what was to be, according to their own natures. About Judah he said:

"Your brothers will praise you. Rulers will descend from you. You will be known as a leader of men."

What Jacob saw in the future for his son Judah, came true in this way:

After wandering in the desert for forty years, the Israelites reached their promised land. They settled in Canaan. Here the land was divided among the Twelve Tribes, named for the twelve sons of Jacob.

One of the first to enter the land of Canaan was the Tribe of Judah, known for its warriors. They settled in the southern part of the land.

The land of Canaan became the Kingdom of Israel. It was ruled first by Saul, then David, then Solomon—the first three Hebrew kings—through almost one hundred years. After King Solomon's death, the land was divided into two separate kingdoms—the northern Kingdom of Israel, and the southern Kingdom of Judah.

The northern kingdom was conquered and it disappeared, and only the kingdom to the south remained to our ancestors. This was the Kingdom of Judah.

The people living in the Kingdom of Judah became known as Judeans. The religion of the Judeans in time was called Judaism. It is from the descendants of Judah, son of Jacob, that we Jews of today get our name.

Although Jacob was old and weak, he saw well what the future held in store for his fourth son. The story is told in the *Book of Genesis,* Chapter 49. Jacob compared Judah to a young lion. That is why the lion became the emblem of the Tribe of Judah.

...AND THE SYMBOL

Today the lion is a favorite decoration on the Torah Mantle, Breastplate, Parokhet, Holy Ark and Hanukkah Menorah. Often the design shows two lions, facing each other with the Tablets of the Law or the Menorah between them.

An interesting note is proviaed by the history of the City of Jerusalem. Judah's descendants ruled our people, and Jerusalem was the Capitol of the Jewish kingdom. The lion of Judah became a symbol of the City of Zion, and is today part of the seal of modern Jerusalem.

Thus an ancient symbol, signifying strength and majesty, lives on in our own day.

SHOFAR

The Trumpet That Isn't a Trumpet

THE STORY . . .

A boy who took care of sheep found that his "Shofar" was missing.

"What is a Shofar?" asked the first man he came to.

"A Shofar is—a Shofar," the boy stammered, for he did not know what else to say.

"Yes, but *what* is it?" the man insisted.

The boy tried to find words. "It is something that *looks* like a Shofar. It *sounds* like a Shofar. It *feels* like a Shofar. That is why we call it a Shofar!" he beamed.

The man looked at him blankly.

Quickly the boy added, "You might say it's something like a trumpet."

"Aha!" declared the man. "Now I understand. But why didn't you say at once that a Shofar is a trumpet?"

"Because—" said the boy, "a Shofar is not a trumpet!"

Although the Shofar, like a trumpet, is blown to make sounds, it is not a trumpet. It is made from the ram's horn, which is somewhat flattened and then hollowed out.

The Shofar was one of the first wind instruments ever used, and is not at all easy to blow. To get a sound out of it, it must be put to the lips in a certain way. The sounds that come out are not at all like the sounds of trumpets or other horns. The sound that comes out of a Shofar is like no other sound in the world.

Three different calls are made on the Shofar: *Tekiah,* a long blast starting on a low note and rising nearly an octave; *Shevarim,* which consists of three shorter notes; and *Teru'ah,* which is made up of nine quick, sharp calls ending with a high note.

The Shofar takes us back to Abraham, who was told by God to substitute a ram for his son Isaac as a sacrifice on the altar.

In ancient days, the sound of the ram's horn was a signal. It called the Israelites together to receive the Torah. Its blast thundered out of a thick cloud hanging over Mount Sinai. The Bible says, "The voice of the horn grew louder and louder" (*Exodus* 19:19).

At another time, its fearsome noise helped the Israelites bring down the walls of Jericho and enter the first city of the Promised Land. The Bible says, "When the people heard the sound of the horn they let out a great shout and the wall fell down flat (*Joshua* 6:20).

In war, its piercing notes were often used to spread an alarm. In peaceful days, its call proclaimed the reign of a new king, and announced the Sabbath, the festivals, and the Jubilee every fiftieth year.

The Torah names Rosh Hashanah, the New Year, as "a day of blowing the horn" (*Numbers* 29:1). Throughout the world, the call of the Shofar in our synagogue on Rosh Hashanah reminds the congregation of the need for doing good and for living an honorable and God-fearing life. The Shofar is also blown once at the end of Yom Kippur, the Day of Atonement.

Jewish tradition tells us that the blast of the Shofar on Rosh Hashanah reaches God Himself. It reminds Him that it is time to judge the deeds of men.

The Shofar and its call are symbols. To every Jewish man, woman, and child the call of the Shofar is a symbol of our people's unity.

SUCCAH

A House for a Free Man

THE STORY . . .

Three slaves escaped from their masters and set out to find freedom in distant places.

"Ah," said one, "I will settle in a big city and build a strong house. I will lock myself in at night, and there I will live in freedom."

The second said, "I will build myself a ship and never touch port where men are slaves. In my ship I will be free!"

The third young man listened thoughtfully. "I will search for freedom, too," he said. "But it won't be for a house that holds me a prisoner. Nor will it be a ship that is afraid to make port. I will search for a place where, even though I may live in a hut of twigs and branches, I will sleep soundly without fear of anyone. Then will I rejoice in my freedom."

. . . AND THE SYMBOL

The festival of Succot, which begins on the fifteenth day of the Hebrew month of Tishri, is called "The Festival of Booths" in the Bible. Succot is the Hebrew word for booths. In *Leviticus* 23:39-40, we read: "When you have gathered in the fruits of the land, you shall keep the feast of the Lord. You shall dwell in booths for seven days."

And on this festival of rejoicing, a "Succah" is built outdoors, and in it the family eats its meals.

The Succah is easily built, for it is a simple frame, covered over with leaves and branches. The Succah is a reminder of the makeshift shelters made of dry palms and branches in which the Israelites lived when they escaped from Egypt and rejoiced in their freedom from slavery. It is as flimsy as an ancient tent made of goatskin, hung over poles, stuck into the ground. It reminds us that our ancestors were the children of Israel who came out of the land of Egypt. During the forty years the Israelites wandered in the desert, they slept and ate in such tents.

Today, when we sit in the booth covered with branches and leaves from which hang fruits of the season, we think of our forefathers. The fruit reminds us of the good things which come to mankind out of the earth. It also reminds us of how dependent we are on God's gifts. But above all, as we sit in the Succah we are reminded of the true meaning of freedom.

The Succah is a symbol of wandering and hardship, and of the freedom that followed slavery. It is a voice from the past, teaching us a lesson for the future.

LULAV AND ETROG

All Together

A ship at sea began to sink and the passengers jumped into a lifeboat. They were still far from land when one of the men began to bore a hole in the bottom of the boat.

"Don't do that!" the others shouted.

"Why not?" said the man. "I am only boring under my own seat."

"Yes," said his comrades, "but when the sea rushes in we will all be drowned with you."

. . . AND THE SYMBOL

Like men in a boat at sea, what one human being does may very well affect the others. The "Lulav" and "Etrog," part of the Succot Festival, remind us how true this is for Jews.

The Bible commands us to take four things—the Etrog (or citron), the Lulav (or palm branch), the Myrtle, and the Willow—and rejoice before God.

The Lulav is waved while prayers of thanksgiving are said. It is waved in six directions. First to the east, then to the south, west, and north, up and down, forward and backward.

The Lulav and Etrog are symbols of thanksgiving for the good things that come out of God's earth.

The Lulav is made up of a branch of the palm tree, three twigs of myrtle, and two willow branches, all tied together in a bundle. The Lulav and Etrog together make up *Arba Minim,* or "four kinds."

Why do we use these "four kinds?" Our rabbis of old thought of several reasons. One explanation is that the Etrog is like the heart, without which man cannot live. The Lulav is the spine; the myrtle is the eye, and the willow leaves are lips. Together they declare that a human being should serve God with all his soul and body.

According to another explanation, the "four kinds" stand for four types of Jews.

The Etrog tastes good and smells sweet and stands for Jews who study the Torah and do good deeds.

The palm's dates have taste, but no fragrance. They stand for Jews who study the Torah but do not good deeds.

The twig of myrtle has no taste, but it has fragrance. It stands for the Jews who do not study the Torah, but who do good deeds.

The willow has no taste and no fragrance. It stands for Jews who neither study the Torah nor do good deeds.

The lesson we learn is that all of us are tied together in one bond of brotherhood. Each helps the other and supplies what the other cannot. Like the men in the lifeboat, we depend on each other.

The Lulav and Etrog are a symbol of Jewish peoplehood.

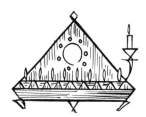

HANUKKAH MENORAH

The best Merchandise

מנורת
חנוכה
58

A teacher of the Torah on board a ship full of merchants was asked, "And what is your merchandise?"

"The best merchandise in the world," he answered, and would say no more.

Curious, the others looked into the hold of the ship, but could find nothing but that which they themselves had brought on board. They winked at each other and laughed at the merchandise of the teacher of the Torah.

The ship was wrecked and all its freight was lost. The passengers barely escaped with their lives, and huddled together in a lifeboat that would take them to land.

The merchants moaned over their loss. "I have lost everything," said one. "Everything I value is at the bottom of the sea!"

The teacher said nothing, and remembering the "best" merchandise, the merchant asked, "Didn't your merchandise go down with the ship?"

The Jew shook his head. "I have not lost what I value most," he said.

A Jew's most prized possession is his faith. Jewish faith is belief in God and Torah. His best merchandise is his heritage of Judaism.

Time and time again, from the beginning of the world, Jews have been separated from their possessions. But they could not be separated from their beliefs.

King Antiochus tried to separate Jews from their worship of God. He ordered them to bow down to idols. He killed hundreds of Jews to show what would happen if all Jews did not obey. But he could not kill their faith in God and Torah. That happened over two thousand years ago, in 168 B.C.E. It marked the first time in history that a people had taken up arms to defend its religious freedom.

Judah Maccabee led this fight for the freedom to believe in God and the right to live by His laws. Three years after the king's army had entered Jerusalem and taken over the Holy Temple, Judah and his Jewish fighters took it back again.

The lamp used at Hanukkah is a special Menorah. The Hanukkah Menorah has branches for eight candles and one more for a Shammash, or helper. This extra candle is used to light the others.

On the first night of Hanukkah, the Shammash is used to light one candle. On the second night of Hanukkah it is used to light two candles, and so forth through the eight nights of Hanukkah.

Before kindling the lights a prayer is said, thanking God for His miracles done for us in days gone by and in our times.

. . . AND THE SYMBOL

In celebration, the Maccabees cleansed the Temple, restored worship, relighted the Menorah, and celebrated the first "Hanukkah." Hanukkah is a Hebrew word meaning dedication.

A legend is told about that Hanukkah. When the moment came to light the lamp, no supply of oil could be found. The priests hurried off to prepare new oil. The others went ahead with their prayers and the Hanukkah ceremony. They lit the scant bit of oil they found as a symbol of their faith.

It is said that a miracle happened. For the oil, which was hardly enough to last one day, burned steadily through eight days!

That is why we celebrate Hanukkah for eight days.

The Hanukkah lights are a symbol. They remind the Jewish people not so much of the miracle of the lamp which burned without oil, but of the miracle of the strength of their faith in God. It reminds them of their "best merchandise." As Judah Maccabee fought for the right to his faith, so did all the Jews who came after him.

Today, at Hanukkah time, on the twenty-fifth day of Kislev on the Jewish calendar, the first Hanukkah light is lit. In Israel, the first Hanukkah light is lit in the village in which Judah lived two thousands years ago. It is called Modi'in. From there it is carried to Tel Aviv where a big Hanukkah Menorah is lit.

The Hanukkah lights glow every year in all the cities of the world where Jews live. They glow also in the hearts of all of us who believe that freedom to live and learn under God is every man's right and cannot be taken away.

HANUKKAH DRAYDEL

The Fast Thinker

THE STORY . . .

A wealthy man lost all his money overnight in a business deal. A friend who came to comfort him in his loss found him heartily eating a big dinner.

In surprise, the friend exclaimed, "Only yesterday a terrible thing happened to you, and today you act as if nothing had taken place! How can you sit there so calmly?"

"You see," said the man who had lost all his money, "I am a Jew, and I have had to learn to think fast. And, having learned to think fast, I have worried in one moment as much as another would worry in a year."

"Thinking fast" has often saved the lives of men threatened by danger. In the time of King Antiochus, any Jew caught studying the Torah instead of praying to idols was immediately killed. But Jews prayed in secret, even though it was often necessary to think fast in order not to lose their lives.

According to an old legend, a favorite way was to gather together in little groups to pray. When the soldiers rushed in, they would find only a circle of Jews playing a harmless game with a little spinning top. When the soldiers left, the Jews put the little toy away, and went on with their praying.

. . . AND THE SYMBOL

The spinning top came to be called a "Draydel." In Israel it is called a *"Svivon."* Draydels are made by the thousands today. At Hanukkah every Jewish child has one.

The Hanukkah Draydel has four sides. Each side bears a Hebrew letter: They are: *Nun, Gimel, Hay,* and *Shin.* These letters stand for the Hebrew words—*Nes Gadol Hayah Sham,* which says in Hebrew: A great miracle happened there.

סביבון

63

The Draydel is used to play a spinning game. It is played today in the same way it was played in ancient times. When it is spinned so that a *Nun* comes up, the player wins nothing from the pot. With *Gimel,* the player takes all. *Hay* means the player gets half. *Shin* tells the player to put into the pot.

The Draydel game reminds the players of the fast thinking of those ancient heroes. The Draydel game is played every Hanukkah as a symbol of victory.

MEGILLAH

The Fur Coat

THE STORY . . .

An old man who knew he did not have long to live sold everything he owned for money to carry to his children. The only thing he bought for himself was a fine fur coat for his journey.

On the way he met a poor man who shook with the cold and who had no coat. The old man took off his fine coat and gave it away.

"It is a Mitzvah!" whispered the poor man gratefully, as he wrapped himself in the warm coat.

As the old man continued on his way, a band of robbers overtook him. They saw that he shivered in the cold and they went right past him.

With a pocket full of gold, the old man went safely on his way.

AND THE SYMBOL

A "Mitzvah" is a good deed. Every commandment of the Lord is a Mitzvah. The only reward for a Mitzvah is the good that comes of doing it.

On Purim, it is a Mitzvah to read or listen to the "Megillah." Megillah is Hebrew for scroll. The Purim Megillah contains the story of Esther.

The Book of Esther is not part of the Five Books of Moses, but it is part of our Bible. The Bible is divided into three parts. The first is the Torah, or the Five Books of Moses. The second is The Prophets. The third is called The Writings. The Book of Esther is part of The Writings.

On Purim the story of Esther is not read from a printed book of the Bible. It is read from a parchment scroll. This scroll is known as the Megillah of Esther.

The Megillah is read in the synagogue after the evening service on the eve of Purim and again on the morning of Purim.

The Megillah tells the story of Esther, who long ago saved our people from the hands of an evil man named Haman who wished to destroy us all. It is a tale full of excitement and hairbreadth escapes, and we have never grown weary of hearing it.

Very often, the Megillah is beautifully illustrated with scenes from the story. Sometimes the borders are decorated with flowers, birds, animals or graceful designs.

The Megillah is a symbol. The parchment and the handwritten words remind us that this is an old, old holiday. We remember that Purim recalls the downfall of a tyrant, and we realize that hate without reason holds its own punishment, just as a Mitzvah is its own reward.

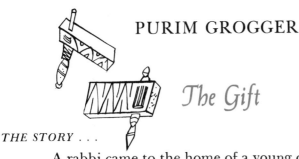

PURIM GROGGER

The Gift

THE STORY . . .

A rabbi came to the home of a young couple to see their new baby. He carried with him a neatly wrapped gift for the child.

The young mother, politely pretending not to see the big package under his arm, showed her visitor all the gifts the baby had received . . . gifts that made music, and gifts that taught words, and gifts that rolled, and gifts that walked. And as she showed all the beautiful things to the rabbi, she wondered what was in the package under his arm. Surely it would be as fine a gift as any her child had received.

Finally, the rabbi held out the bulky package. "I have chosen a gift for your child that will help him grow up," said the rabbi.

When he had gone, the young woman eagerly unwrapped the gift. She took off the ribbon, removed the fancy paper, and carefully unrolled the tissue.

She looked at the gift in surprise. The card said, "Break me if you wish." The young mother picked up the gift and turned it about. It was nothing but an old clay flower pot, worth only a few pennies.

. . . AND THE SYMBOL

An ancient rabbi in the Talmud advised parents to provide their children with some things of no value, which they could break if they wished. Even in those long-ago days it was recognized that children sometimes need to stamp their feet and shout and break things.

Perhaps this is the reason that Purim is the most popular holiday for children. For Purim is a holiday at which stamping and shouting and making noise is the order of the day.

On every Purim the legend is told how Queen Esther saved the Jewish people from the cruelties of the tyrant, Haman. Hamantashen, cookies in the shape of Haman's three-cornered hat, are eaten with joy and children dress up in costumes and loudly boo Haman and all like him.

At Purim a noisemaker is a favorite symbol. It is called a Grogger because its rasping voice cries "Gr-r-og gr-r-og gr-r-og!"

The grogger belongs to the family of percussion instruments. Percussion instruments are those which must be struck to make a sound. They include drums, cymbals, and bells.

The Grogger began as two instruments—the "bull-roarer" and the "scraper." The bull-roarer, of wood, was twirled to make a noise. The scraper, which was a shell or bone or gourd, was scraped to make a noise. The rattle of the Grogger combines both of these sounds. The Grogger is nothing more than a clacker on a handle. When it is whirled around in the air, it makes much noise.

And that is why we use it on Purim. In *Deuteronomy* 25:19 the Israelites are told to "blot out the remembrance of Amalek." Amalek was the name of the first enemy of our ancestors after they had left Egypt. The Grogger at Purim strikes a note of confidence. It shouts down all Hamans (enemies like Amalek) and blots them out. The Grogger was used for this Purim purpose as far back as the 13th century in France and Germany.

In some countries, Haman's name was written on the soles of the shoes, which were rubbed on the floor during the Megillah reading. Thus was Haman's name actually wiped out.

In synagogues today, the Megillah with its story of Esther and Mordecai and Haman is read aloud on Purim. The Grogger is whirled noisily at every mention of the name of Haman.

The sound of the Grogger is a sign of Purim. The noise it makes is a happy noise. It says "Down with all tyrants," and "Long live liberty!"

The Grogger is the symbol of Purim, a fun-filled, gift-gay holiday.

MATZAH

The Taste Test

THE STORY . . .

Before Passover, a young rabbi brought to his students a square package, wrapped in a white napkin.

"We will conduct a test," he announced. Folding back the napkin, he revealed two squares of "Matzah." He broke one of the Matzot into several pieces and gave each student a piece.

"Now," he said, "eat the piece of Matzah and tell me what you taste."

Mystified, the first student tasted the Matzah.

"What does it taste like to you?" asked the teacher.

The boy swallowed. "It tastes like Matzah to me," he said with a grin.

The rabbi nodded. He turned to the second boy. "And to you?"

Slowly the boy tasted, and chewed, and swallowed. Then he shook his head. "I don't know," he said.

The third boy could find no special taste either. At that the pupils gave up.

But the young rabbi didn't seem to be displeased. "Now we will read about the beginnings of Passover and then we will make the test again."

Wondering what this was all about, the boys bent over their books. The clock ticked on, and the story of Moses and the Hebrews in slavery in Egypt rolled before their minds. The ten plagues, the escape, and the crossing of the Red Sea to freedom.

. . . AND THE SYMBOL

When the Hebrews hurried out of Egypt, they took with them everything they owned, the boys read. They took their sheep and their goats. They took the tools of their trades, the pots and pans of their hearths, the quilts from their beds. They took even the dough set to rise, for they needed food to give them strength as they fled. They carried their clothes in bundles on their shoulders and on top of that they placed the bread dough.

Led by Moses, the Israelites moved as quickly as they could out of Egypt. The hot sun beat down on the dough as they carried it along with them and baked it. The result was a flat dry biscuit which tasted not at all like bread. Thus were prepared the Matzot which were to become such an important symbol in our celebration of Passover.

It was the first bit of food they had eaten since they had left Egypt. And as they stopped and rested, and ate, they knew they were no longer slaves . . .

Carefully, the rabbi broke up the second Matzah. Silently he passed it around. "Now eat this," he said. "Eat it and tell me what you taste."

Thoughtfully, the boys ate their Matzah.

"It tastes like freedom," said the first one in wonder. And the others nodded.

Today at Pesah, the holiday which commemorates that flight of the Hebrews out of Egypt, Matzah is always eaten instead of bread. The Matzah is baked thin and crisp. It is made, as that first Matzah was, without leavening.

The eating of unleavened bread, or Matzah, for seven days in the month of Nisan is commanded in the Bible, *Exodus* 12:15. Now, Passover is observed for eight days. (Reform Jews do not observe the eighth day.)

The eating of Matzah on Passover is a symbol. It reminds us of our ancestors who were once slaves in Egypt.

MATZAH

We remember the bread our fathers baked in haste when they left the land of Pharaoh. And as we eat the flat, dry unleavened bread, we can taste, as those brave Israelites did, the triumph of freedom.

CUP OF ELIJAH

Waiting for Elijah

THE STORY . . .

A poor woman came crying to her rabbi. Her daughter was about to be married but she had no candlesticks to place on the table. She was afraid that her future son-in-law and his family would think she did not care enough to make the bridal table gay and festive.

So the rabbi gave her his best silver candlesticks.

When Friday evening came around, the rabbi's wife went to light the Sabbath candles. To her surprise she discovered that her beautiful silver candlesticks were gone.

"Thieves!" she cried. "Someone has stolen our candlesticks!"

"No one has stolen our candlesticks," said the rabbi.

"Then where are they?" asked the rabbi's wife.

Gently, her husband told her, "They have gone to light our way into the world-to-come."

. . . AND THE SYMBOL

Doing good deeds, the Jewish people believe, is the way to make this world a heavenly place. While we believe that souls go to heaven, we do our best to create a heaven here on earth. We pray for a time to come when all people will live together in this world in peace and understanding.

We look forward to this better world-to-come, and call it the time of the Messiah. "Messiah" is Hebrew for "one anointed with oil"—the ancient way of dedicating a man to a special service or office. The kings of Israel, for example, were anointed by prophets.

During long centuries of exile from Palestine, our ancestors prayed for the arrival of a Messiah—a deliverer who would defeat Israel's enemies and lead the Jewish people back to the Holy Land.

We believe that when the Messiah comes all people will understand each other and respect each other. In this way peace will come to the world.

In Jewish tradition, when peace comes to the world, Elijah will be the one to bring the news. Elijah the prophet will announce the coming of the Messiah.

In Jewish tradition, Elijah also became a comforter of the poor and the suffering. He was said to appear, sometimes in disguise, when the need was greatest. So people yearned to see him, and never so much as on Passover, when thoughts of freedom were in all hearts and on all lips.

To this day, at the Seder table on Passover, a special cup is filled with wine in honor of the Prophet. This is called the Cup of Elijah. At one point in the Seder service we open the door wide and "welcome" Elijah in.

The welcome cup of wine for Elijah is set out every Passover in the hope that the time of his coming will be that very year.

The Cup of Elijah is a symbol of hope for a better world to come.

HUPPAH
(Wedding Canopy)

A Princess Who Always Said No

THE STORY . . .

A king had a beautiful daughter who said, "No," to every one of the rich young men who asked for her hand in marriage. This troubled the king. One night he dreamed that his daughter would marry the poorest youth in all of Israel.

To make sure that such a thing would not really happen, he sent his daughter to live in a castle, high on a hill, surrounded by a great wall. He kept the keys to the castle in his pocket at all times.

One night while the king was sleeping soundly, a young man lost his way on the road near the castle. Since he had neither horse nor carriage, he sat down by the side of the road when night came and went to sleep.

While he slept, a huge bird picked him up, and flew off with him. But the weight of the young man became too much for the bird, and it set him down on the roof of the palace and flew away.

Naturally, the princess found him and fell in love with him and wanted to marry him.

The king was not at all angry when he discovered this. He felt that if this happened after all his efforts to prevent it, then it was meant to be.

. . AND THE SYMBOL

Marriage is sacred. To the Jewish people, marriage ceremonies are the happiest of all religious occasions. Among most Jewish families, the wedding day begins with the setting up of a "Huppah."

A Huppah is a wedding canopy. Canopy means covering. The Huppah is a square of cloth and is held up at the corners by four poles. Often a large prayer shawl, a Tallit, is used as the canopy for the Huppah. The bride and groom stand under the Huppah during the marriage ceremony.

Among the legends which have grown up about Jewish ceremonies and customs are many about the origin of the Huppah. One legend says that when a boy was born to a Jewish family in ancient times, a cedar tree was planted. And for a girl, a cypress. The tree grew as the child grew. And the branches of the tree were cut to be used as poles for the Huppah at the marriage ceremony.

Another legend says that the Huppah represents the litter, or chair with a tent-like covering over it, on which the bride was carried to the ceremony in long-ago days.

But many people think that the custom of setting up a wedding canopy over the bride and groom comes from the ancient days when the Israelites lived in tents. A special tent was usually set aside for a bridal couple. When Jews no longer lived in tents, but in houses in cities, the custom of having a tent for the bridal couple was kept in the marriage ceremony with a canopy. The Huppah made a tent over the bride and groom.

The Huppah today is thought of as a symbol of the one roof under which the new couple will build a Jewish home.

And now, Israel,
what does the Lord your God require of you,
but to respect the Lord your God,
to walk in all His ways, and to love Him,
and to serve the Lord your God
with all your heart and with all your soul;
to keep for your good the commandments
of the Lord,
and His statutes,
which I command you this day.

DEUTERONOMY 10:12

AN AFTERWORD

Many books have a preface, introduction, or foreword. This book is unusual because it has an afterword, summing up all that has gone before. Our afterword begins with a question:

What Makes You a Jew?

What's in a name?

Quite a lot! Judaism is much more than a name; it is a way to live. To be born a Jew doesn't mean that you were chosen for any extra privileges. It means you belong to a family of people who long ago accepted a responsibility. The Law was given by God to the Jews—but it is up to each Jew to keep it.

What makes you a Jew? The answer has two parts: the fact that you recognize yourself as a Jew; and the fact that you fulfill the duties of a Jew. To be born a Jew is not enough. To love good, to seek wisdom, and to think of your fellow man—all these are part of being a Jew.

To be a Jew means you must live the Jewish way of life. The symbols of Judaism described in this book will help to show you what that way is.

Building on the spiritual strength stored up by your fathers and forefathers over thousands of years, you can help create a world in which people of different colors, creeds, and nationalities will live together in understanding.

SOURCES OF STORIES

Most of the Stories used in this book have been adapted from Jewish folk literature. Those sources are as follows:

"The Trumpet That Isn't a Trumpet"—adapted from "A Rosh Hashonah Joke," Sept. 10, 1926, issue of *The Jewish Tribune for Juniors.*

"The Promise"—adapted from a tale from the Midrash, Page 121, *A Rabbinic Anthology,* C. G. Montefiore and H. Loewe, The World Publishing Company.

"The Fish Who Were Afraid"—adapted from a parable of "The Fox and the Fishes," page 136, *A Rabbinic Anthology,* C. G. Montefiore and H. Loewe, The World Publishing Company.

"The Old Man and the Fig Tree"—adapted from "Hadrian and the Aged Planter," page 150, *The Jewish Caravan,* Leo W. Schwarz, Holt, Rinehart and Winston.

"The Question"—from "Why Noodles are Noodles," page 303, *A Treasury of Jewish Folklore,* Nathan Ausubel, Crown Publishers.

"Moonbeams in a Barrel"—adapted from a Helm tale, page 320, *The Jewish Caravan,* Leo W. Schwarz.

"The Rabbi and the Robber"—adapted from "My Brother Kitov," page 487, *The Talmudic Anthology,* Louis I. Newman, Behrman House, Inc.

"The Best Merchandise"—adapted from "Torah is the Best Sehora," page 495, *The Talmudic Anthology,* Louis I. Newman, Behrman House, Inc.

"The Fast Thinker"—adapted from "Concentrated Anxiety," page 127, *The Hasidic Anthology,* Louis I. Newman, Bloch Publishing Company.

"The Secret Ingredient"—adapted from "Sabbath Spice," page 192, *The Rabbinic Anthology,* C. G. Montefiore and H. Loewe.

"The World and the Vineyard"—adapted from "A Tale of Satan and Noah," page 527, *A Rabbinic Anthology,* C. G. Montefiore and H. Loewe, The World Publishing Company.

"The Ending of the Song"—adapted, page 23, *The Hasidic Anthology,* Louis I. Newman, Bloch Publishing Co.

"A House for a Free Man"—adapted from "The Escaped Prisoner," page 450, *The Talmudic Anthology,* Louis I. Newman, Behrman House, Inc.

"All Together"—adapted from a Talmud tale, page 6, *A Book of Jewish Thoughts,* J. H. Hertz, Bloch Publishing Co.

"The Gift"—adapted from "The Care of Children," page 71, *The Talmudic Anthology,* Louis I. Newman, Behrman House, Inc.

"Waiting for Elijah"—adapted from "Tapers to Heaven," page 507, *Treasury of Jewish Folklore,* Nathan Ausubel, Crown Publishers.

"A Gift for a Gift"—adapted from a Talmudic tale, page 133, *The Rabbinic Anthology,* C. G. Montefiore and H. Loewe, The World Publishing Company.

"The Prayer Shawl"—adapted from "Prayer Before Prayer," page 159, *A Treasury of Jewish Folklore,* Nathan Ausubel, Crown Publishers.

"The Princess Who Always Said No"—adapted from a tale from the Midrash, page 275, *The Wisdom of Israel,* Lewis Browne, The Modern Library.

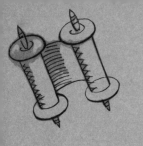